Dedicated To:
The Karr Family

Written By: Abigail Gartland

I was born in Tarsus in the year 5.

When I was a young boy, I was actually named Saul.

In my early life as a young man, I spent my days as a Pharisee.

That means, I believed in God the Father, but did not believe that Jesus was God's son.

One day, I was walking on the road and a very bright ligh shined down on me.

The light was so bright that I couldn't see a thing. I looked around for help and heard a voice from the sky.

I was very scared and heard the voice say, "Saul, Saul, why are you against me?"

I was very scared and asked
"Who are you, sir?"
The voice spoke and
said "I am Jesus!"

After the light faced away, I could not see, but I went toward the town of Damascus where the voice of Jesus told me to go.

On my way to Damascus, a man met me and said, "Saul, the Lord has sent me, that you may regain your sign and be filled with the Holy Spirit."

After the man spoke those words, I was able to see again!

The man baptized me, and I changed my name to Paul to live as a new man who followed Jesus.

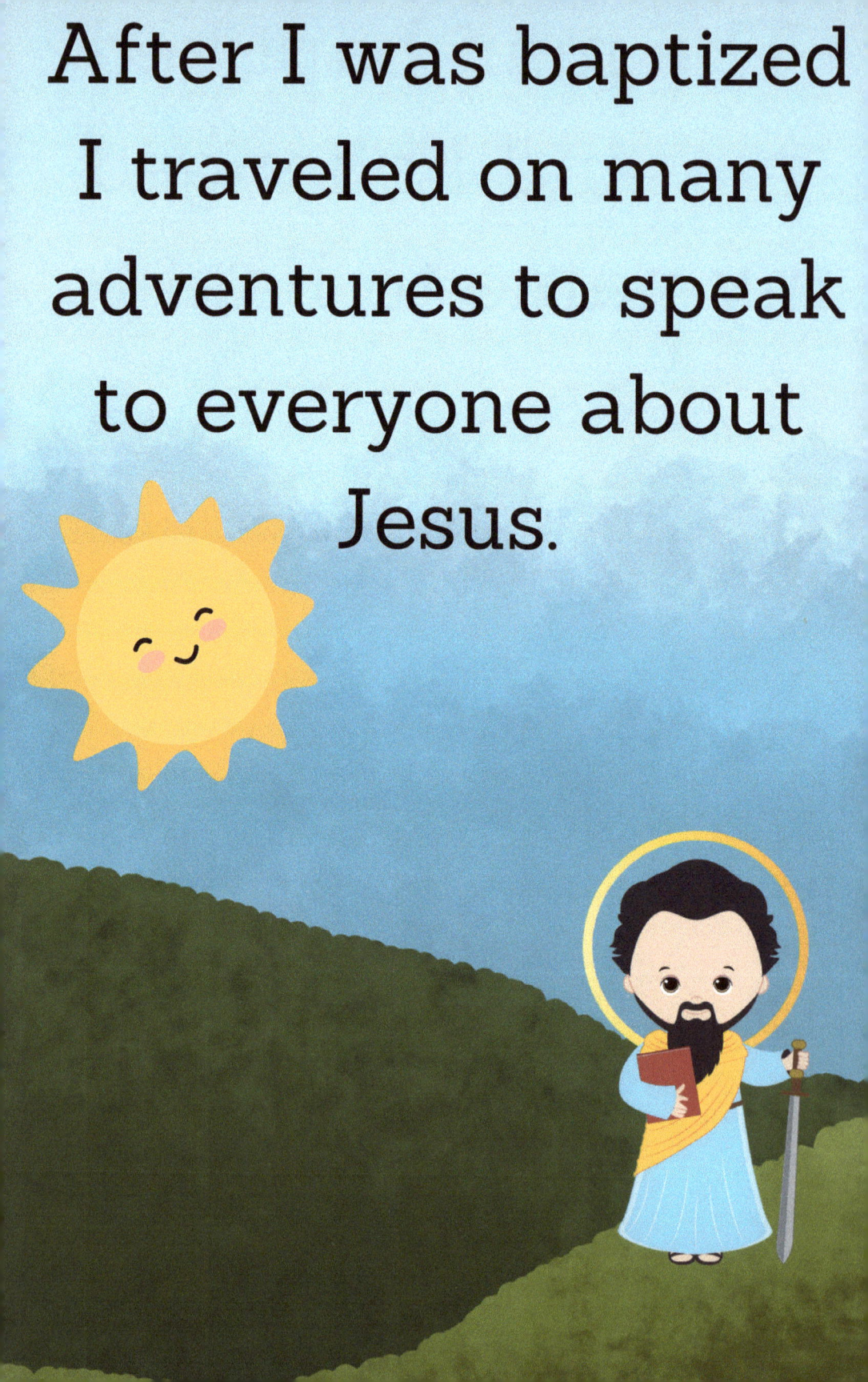
After I was baptized I traveled on many adventures to speak to everyone about Jesus.

I shared the message of Jesus of how He loves us so much through the letters I wrote.

I wrote more than 10 books in the bible, and I shared my teachings with everyone I saw on my journeys!

Do you want to be more like me?

You can celebrate my feast day with me on June 29th.

I am the patron saint of adventures, religion teachers, and Christians.

I pray for you every day of your life.

St. Paul, pray for us!

Copyright:

Clipart:  © PentoolPixie © LimeandKiwiDesigns
Licensed purchased: 1/10/2024

About the Author

Abigail Gartland

I love the saints and I love my faith. The idea for sharing the stories of the saints with little ones came when my dear friends were expecting their first baby. I wanted to create something as unique and special as our friendship. Each book is dedicated to very special people and groups who have enriched my faith in different ways. I am blessed to write these stories and appreciate the unending support of my family and friends. When I am not writing, I am a middle school teacher. I hope you enjoy these stories. I pray for each and every person who opens one of my books to learn more about the saints.

Abbie